Keto Diet Recipes

for Carb Lovers

Discover Simple, Quick, And Easy Cookbook to Burn Fat, Increase Energy and Lose Weight Quickly

Benedict Holland

This declaration is deemed fair and valid by both the American Bar Association and the Committee of Publishers Association and is legally binding throughout the United States.

Furthermore, the transmission, duplication, or reproduction of any of the following work including specific information will be considered an illegal act irrespective of if it is done electronically or in print. This extends to creating a secondary or tertiary copy of the work or a recorded copy and is only allowed with the express written consent from the Publisher. All additional right reserved.

The information in the following pages is broadly considered a truthful and accurate account of facts and as such, any inattention, use, or misuse of the information in question by the reader will render any resulting actions solely under their purview. There are no scenarios in which the publisher or the original author of this work can be in any fashion deemed liable for any hardship or damages that may befall them after undertaking information described herein.

Additionally, the information in the following pages is intended only for informational purposes and should thus be thought of as universal. As befitting its nature, it is presented without assurance regarding its prolonged validity or interim quality. Trademarks that are mentioned are done without written consent and can in no way be considered an endorsement from the trademark holder.

Table of Contents

MEAT

1.   Boston Pork Caritas

Preparation time: 15 minutes

Cooking time: 8 hours

Servings: 2

Ingredients:

- 1 (8 lb.) Boston pork butt

- 1 large onion

- 2 tbsp. butter/bacon grease

- 4 tbsp. minced garlic

- 2 tbsp. of each:

- 2tbsp.Chili powder

- 2tbsp.Thyme

- 2tbsp.Cumin

- Pepper

- Salt

- 1 c. water

Directions

1. Grease the slow cooker with the butter/oil. Slice and add the onion along with the minced garlic to the pot.

2. Remove most of the fat from the meat and slice in a crisscross pattern on the top. Combine the spices and rub the meat. (If there's any left, just add it to the top of the garlic and onions.)

3. Place the meat into the pot and add the water. Cook for eight hours (1 hr. per lb.) on the high setting.

4. You will know it's done when it falls off the bone.

5.

Nutrition: Calories: 324; Total fat: 9; Protein: 17 g; Carbs: 4 gFiber: 12 g

2.   Chinese-Style Pork Hock

Preparation time: 15 minutes

Cooking time: 2 hours

Servings: 2

Ingredients:

- 1 lb. pork hock

- 1/3cup-Soy sauce

- 1/3cup Shaoxing cooking wine

- 1/4cup Rice vinegar

- 1/4cup Soy sauce

- 1/4cup Splendid/favorite keto sweetener

- 1/2 c. shiitake mushrooms

- 1/3 med. onion

- 2 crushed cloves of garlic

- 1tsp. Chinese five-spice

- 1tsp.Oregano

- 1 tbsp. butter/coconut oil

Directions

1. Warm up the slow cooker using high heat setting.

2. Arrange the onions in a skillet to fry.

3. Fill up another saucepan with water to boil the mushrooms.

4. Also, set up a pan to sear the hock using the butter. Brown the hock in the butter until crispy. Toss all of the ingredients into the slow cooker, mixing well. Let it cook on the high setting for two hours. Stir and

continue cooking for another two hours on the low heat setting.

5. Transfer the pork from the cooker and debone. Slice and add it back to the sauce. Stir and serve with a favorite side dish.

Nutrition: Calories: 256; Total fat: 8; Protein: 21 g; Carbs: 5 gFiber: 12 g

3.   Parmesan Honey Pork Loin Roast

Preparation time: 10 minutes

Cooking time: 6 hours

Servings: 2-8

Ingredients:

- 3-pound pork loin

- 2/3 Cup grated parmesan cheese

- Soy sauce

- 1 tablespoon oregano

- Basil

- Garlic

- Olive oil

- Salt

- 2 tablespoons cornstarch

- 1/4 cup chicken broth

Directions:

1. Spray your slow cooker with olive oil or nonstick cooking spray.

2. Place the pork loin in the slow cooker.

3. In a small mixing bowl, combine the cheese, honey, soy sauce, oregano, basil, garlic, olive oil, and salt. Stir with a fork to combine well, then pour over the pork loin.

4. Cook on low for 5–6 hours or until roast is done.

5. Remove the pork loin and put on a serving platter.

6. Pour the juices from the slow cooker into a small saucepan. You can strain out the bits if you like, but it is good like it is.

7. Create slurry by mixing the cornstarch into the chicken broth and whisking until smooth.

8. Bring the contents of the saucepan to a boil, then whisk in the slurry, and let simmer until thickened. Pour over the pork loin and serve.

Nutrition:

Calories 448,

Fat 15,

Carbs 1.8,

Protein 32

4. Corned Beef

Preparation time: 10 minutes

Cooking time: 8 hours

Servings: 2

Ingredients:

- 1-pound corned beef
- 1 teaspoon peppercorns
- 1 teaspoon chili flakes
- 1 teaspoon mustard seeds
- 1 bay leaf
- 1 teaspoon salt
- 1 oz. bacon fat
- garlic cloves
- 1 cup water

- 1 tablespoon butter

Directions:

1. Mix the peppercorns, chili flakes, mustard seeds, and salt in the bowl.

2. Then rub the corned beef with the spice mixture well.

3. Peel the garlic and place it in the slow cooker.

4. Add the corned beef.

5. Add water, butter, and bay leaf.

6. Add the bacon fat and close the lid.

7. Cook the corned beef for 8 hours on Low.

8. When the corned beef is cooked, discard the bay leaf, then transfer the beef to a plate and cut into servings.

9. Enjoy!

Nutrition: Calories 178, Fat 13.5, Fiber 0.3, Carbs 1.3, Protein 12.2

5.   Spare Ribs

Preparation time: 10 minutes

Cooking time: 8 hours

Servings: 2

Ingredients:

- 1-pound pork loin ribs

- 1 teaspoon olive oil

- 1 teaspoon minced garlic

- 1/4 teaspoon cumin

- 1/4 teaspoon chili powder

- 1 tablespoon butter

- 1 tablespoons water

Directions:

1. Mix the olive oil, minced garlic, cumin, and chili flakes in a bowl.

2. Melt the butter and add to the spice mixture.

3. Stir it well and add water. Stir again.

4. Then rub the pork ribs with the spice mixture generously and place the ribs in the slow cooker.

5. Close the lid and cook the ribs for 8 hours on Low.

6. When the ribs are cooked, serve them immediately!

Nutrition: Calories 203, Fat 14.1, Fiber 0.6,

Carbs 10, Protein 9.8

6. Pork Shoulder

Preparation time: 25 minutes

Cooking time: 7 hours

Servings: 2

Ingredients:

- 1-pound pork shoulder

- 2 cups water

- 1 onion, peeled

- 2 garlic cloves, peeled

- 1 teaspoon peppercorns

- 1 teaspoon chili flakes

- 1/2 teaspoon paprika

- 1 teaspoon turmeric

- 1 teaspoon cumin

Directions:

1. Sprinkle the pork shoulder with the peppercorns, chili flakes, paprika, turmeric, and cumin.

2. Stir it well and let it sit for 15 minutes to marinate.

3. Transfer the pork shoulder to the slow cooker.

4. Add water and peeled the onion.

5. Add garlic cloves and close the lid.

6. Cook the pork shoulder for 7 hours on Low.

7. Remove the pork shoulder from the slow cooker and serve!

Nutrition: Calories 234, Fat 16.4, Fiber 0.7, Carbs 2.8, Protein 18

7. Lamb Chops

Preparation time: 15 minutes

Cooking time: 3 hours

Servings: 2

Ingredients:

- 1oz. lamb chops
- 1 tablespoon tomato puree
- 1/2 teaspoon cumin
- 1/2 teaspoon ground coriander
- 1 teaspoon garlic powder
- 1 teaspoon butter
- 1tablespoons water

Directions:

1. Mix the tomato puree, cumin, ground coriander, garlic powder, and water in the bowl.

2. Brush the lamb chops with the tomato puree mixture on each side and let marinate for 20 minutes.

3. Toss the butter in the slow cooker.

4. Add the lamb chops and close the lid.

5. Cook the lamb chops for 3 hours on High.

6. Transfer the cooked lamb onto serving plates and enjoy!

Nutrition: Calories 290, Fat 12.5, Fiber 0.4, Carbs 2, Protein 40.3

8. Rosemary Leg of Lamb

Preparation time: 15 minutes

Cooking time: 7 hours

Servings: 2

Ingredients:

- 2-pound leg of lamb
- 1 onion
- 2 cups water
- 1 garlic clove, peeled
- 1 tablespoon mustard seeds
- 1 teaspoon salt
- 1/2 teaspoon turmeric
- 1 teaspoon ground black pepper

Directions:

1. Chop the garlic clove and combine it with the mustard seeds, turmeric, black pepper, and salt.

2. Peel the onion and grate it.

3. Mix the grated onion and spice mixture.

4. Rub the leg of lamb with the grated onion mixture.

5. Put the leg of lamb in the slow cooker and cook it for 7 hours on Low.

6. Serve the cooked meal!

Nutrition: Calories 225,

Fat 8.7,

Fiber 0.6,

Carbs 2.2,

Protein 32.4

SNACKS

9.   Zucchini Tots

Preparation Time: 10 minutes

Cooking Time: 20 minutes

Serve: 4

Ingredients:

- 5 cups zucchini, grated and squeeze out all liquid

- ½ tsp garlic powder ½ tsp dried oregano

- ½ cup parmesan cheese, grated

- ½ cup cheddar cheese, shredded

- 2 eggs, lightly beaten

- Pepper Salt

Directions:

1. Preheat the oven to 400 F.

2. Spray a baking tray with cooking spray and put aside.

3. Add all ingredients into the bowl and blend until well combined.

4. Make small tots from the zucchini mixture and place onto the prepared baking tray.

5. Bake in a preheated oven for 15-20 minutes.

6. Serve and luxuriate in.

Nutrition:

Calories 353

Fat 23.1 g

Carbohydrates 9.5 g

Sugar 2.8 g

Protein 32.1 g

Cholesterol 157 mg

10. Avocado Yogurt Dip

Preparation Time: 5 minutes

Cooking Time: 5 minutes

Serve: 4

Ingredients:

- 2 avocados

- 1 lime juice

- 3 garlic cloves, minced

- ½ cup Greek yogurt

- Pepper Salt

Directions:

1. Scoop out avocado flesh using the spoon and place it during a bowl.

2. Mash avocado flesh using the fork.

3. Add remaining ingredients and stir to mix.

4. Serve and luxuriate in.

Nutrition: Calories 139 Fat 11 g Carbohydrates

9 g Protein 4 g Sugar 2 g Cholesterol 15 mg

11. Keto Macadamia Hummus

Preparation Time: 10 minutes

Cooking Time: 5 minutes Serve: 8

Ingredients:

- 1 cup macadamia nuts, soaked in water for overnight, drained and rinsed

- 1 ½ tbsp tahini

- 2 tbsp water

- 2 tbsp fresh lime juice

- 2 garlic cloves

- 1/8 tsp cayenne pepper

- Pepper Salt

Directions:

1. Add all ingredients into the food processor and process until smooth.

2. Serve and enjoy.

Nutrition: Calories 138 Fat 14.2 g Carbohydrates 3.2 g Protein 1.9 g Sugar 1.9 g Cholesterol 0mg

12. Easy & Perfect Meatballs

Preparation Time: 10 minutes

Cooking Time: 20 minutes Serve: 8

Ingredients:

- 1 egg, lightly beaten

- 3 garlic cloves, minced

- ½ cup mozzarella cheese, shredded

- ½ cup parmesan cheese, grated

- 1 lb. ground beef

- Pepper Salt

Directions:

1. Preheat the oven to 400 F.

2. Line baking tray with parchment paper and put aside.

3. Add all ingredients into the blending bowl and blend until well combined.

4. Make small balls from meat mixture and place on a prepared baking tray.

5. Bake in a preheated oven for 20 minutes.

6. Serve and luxuriate in.

Nutrition: Calories 157 Fat 6.7 g Carbohydrates 0.5 g Protein 21.5 g Sugar 0.1 g Cholesterol 80 mg

13. Eggplant Chips

Preparation Time: 10 minutes

Cooking Time: 20 minutes

Serve: 15

Ingredients:

- 1 large eggplant, thinly sliced

- ¼ cup parmesan cheese, grated

- 1 tsp dried oregano

- ¼ tsp dried basil

- ½ tsp garlic powder

- ¼ cup olive oil

- ¼ tsp pepper

- ½ tsp salt

Directions:

1. Preheat the oven to 325 F.

2. Using a small bowl, mix oil, and dried spices.

3. Coat eggplant with oil and spice mixture and arrange eggplant slices on a baking tray.

4. Bake in a preheated oven for 15-20 minutes. Turn halfway through.

5. Remove from oven and sprinkle with cheese.

6. Serve and luxuriate in.

Nutrition:

Calories 77

Fat 5.8 g

Carbohydrates 2 g

Protein 3.5 g

Sugar 0.9 g

Cholesterol 8mg

14. Creamy Crab Dip

Preparation Time: 5 minutes

Cooking Time: 5 minutes

Serve: 16

Ingredients:

- 8 oz crab meat

- ¼ tsp garlic powder

- 2 tbsp green onion, chopped

- 1 tsp Cajun seasoning

- 1 tbsp lime juice

- ¼ cup mayonnaise

- 3.5 oz cream cheese

- ¼ tsp pepper

- ½ tsp salt

Directions:

1. Add all ingredients into the mixing bowl and whisk until well combined.
2. Serve and enjoy.

Nutrition: Calories 49 Fat 3.6 g Carbohydrates 1.4 g Protein 2.3 g Sugar 0.3 g Cholesterol 15 mg

15. Healthy Chicken Fritters

Preparation Time: 10 minutes

Cooking Time: 20 minutes

Serve: 4

Ingredients:

- 1 ½ lbs chicken breast, skinless, boneless, and chopped in small pieces

- 1 tbsp olive oil

- ½ tsp garlic powder

- 2 tbsp fresh parsley, chopped1 ½ tbsp chives, chopped

- 1 ½ tbsp fresh basil, chopped

- 1 cup mozzarella cheese, shredded

- 1/3 cup almond flour

- 2 eggs, lightly beaten

- Pepper Salt

Directions:

1. Add all ingredients except oil into the massive bowl and blend until well combined.
2. Heat oil during a pan over medium heat.
3. Scoop fritter mixture employing a large spoon and transfer it to the pan and cook for 6-8 minutes or until golden brown on each side.
4. Serve and luxuriate in.

Nutrition: Calories 331 Fat 15.9 g Carbohydrates 2.9 g Protein 43 g Sugar 0.6 g Cholesterol 194mg

16. Creamy Mushrooms with Garlic and Thyme

Preparation time: 5 minutes

Cooking time: 15 minutes

Servings: 2

Ingredients:

- 4 Tbsp unsalted butter

- ½ cup onion, chopped

- 1-pound button mushrooms

- 2 tsp garlic, diced

- 1 tbs fresh thyme

- 1 Tbsp parsley, chopped

- ½ tsp salt

- ¼ tsp black pepper

Directions:

1. Melt the butter during a pan. Place the mushrooms into the pan. Add salt and pepper. Cook the mushroom mix for about 5 minutes until they're browned on each side.
2. Add the garlic and thyme. Additionally, sauté the mushrooms for 1-2 minutes. Top them with parsley.

Nutrition: Carbohydrates – 45 g Fat – 8 g Protein – 3 g Calories – 99

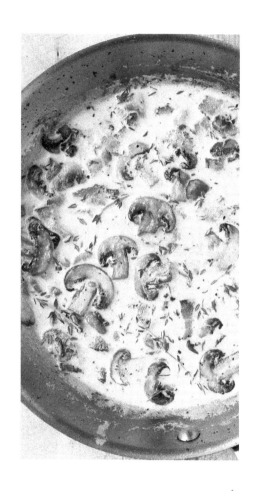

17. Easy Roasted Broccoli

Preparation time: 2 minutes

Cooking time: 19 minutes

Servings: 2

Ingredients:

- 1-pound frozen broccoli, cut into florets

- 3 tsp olive oil

- Sea salt, to taste

Directions:

1. Place broccoli florets on a baking sheet greased with oil and put in the oven (preheated to 400°F).

2. Sprinkle the olive oil over the florets.

3. Cook for 12 minutes. Whisk well and bake for an additional 7 minutes.

Nutrition: Carbohydrates – 8 g Fat – 3 g Protein – 3 g Calories – 58

VEGETABLES

18. Fennel Avgolemono

Preparation time: 10 minutes

Cooking time: 20 minutes

Servings: 2

Ingredients:

- 2tablespoons olive oil
- 1celery stalk, chopped
- 1pound (454 g) fennel bulbs, sliced
- 1garlic clove, minced
- 1bay laurel
- 1thyme sprig
- cups chicken stock
- Sea salt and ground black pepper, to season

- 2eggs

- 1tablespoon freshly squeezed lemon juice

Directions:

1. Heat the olive oil in a heavy-bottomed pot over a medium-high flame. Now, sauté the celery and fennel until they have softened but not browned, about 8 minutes.

2. Add in the garlic, bay laurel, and thyme sprig; continue sautéing until aromatic an additional minute or so.

3. Add the chicken stock, salt, and black pepper to the pot. Bring to a boil. Reduce the heat to medium-low and let it simmer, partially covered, approximately 13 minutes.

4. Discard the bay laurel and then, blend your soup with an immersion blender.

5. Whisk the eggs and lemon juice; gradually pour 2cups of the hot soup into the egg mixture, whisking constantly.

6. Return the soup to the pot and continue stirring for a few minutes or just until thickened. Serve warm.

Nutrition: calories: 85

fat: 6.2g

protein: 2.8g

carbs: 6.0g net

carbs: 3.5g

fiber: 2.5g

19. Spinach and Butternut Squash Stew

Preparation time: 10 minutes

Cooking time: 30 minutes

Servings: 2

Ingredients:

- 2tablespoons olive oil

- 1Spanish onion, peeled and diced

- 1garlic clove, minced

- ½ pound (227 g) butternut squash, diced

- 1celery stalk, chopped

- 3 cups vegetable broth

- Kosher salt and freshly cracked black pepper, to taste

- 4cups baby spinach

- 4 tablespoons sour cream

Directions:

1. Heat the olive oil in a soup pot over a moderate flame. Now, sauté the Spanish onion until tender and translucent.

2. Then, cook the garlic until just tender and aromatic.

3. Stir in the butternut squash, celery, broth, salt, and black pepper. Turn the heat to simmer and let it cook, covered, for 30 minutes.

4. Fold in the baby spinach leaves and cover with the lid; let it sit in the residual heat until the baby spinach wilts completely.

5. Serve dolloped with cold sour cream. Enjoy!

Nutrition: calories: 150 fat: 11.6g protein: 2.5g carbs: 6.8g net carbs: 4.5g fiber: 2.3g

20. Broccoli Cheese

Preparation time: 10 minutes

Cooking time: 15 minutes

Servings: 2

Ingredients:

- 3 tablespoons olive oil

- 1teaspoon garlic, minced

- 1½ pounds (680 g) broccoli florets

- ½ teaspoon flaky salt

- ½ teaspoon ground black pepper

- ½ teaspoon paprika

- ½ cup cream of mushrooms soup

- 6ounces (170 g) Swiss cheese, shredded

Directions:

1. Heat 1tablespoon of the olive oil in a nonstick frying pan over a moderate flame. Then, sauté the garlic until just tender and fragrant.

2. Preheat your oven to 390ºF (199ºC). Now, brush the sides and bottom of a casserole dish with 1tablespoon of olive oil.

3. Parboil the broccoli in salted water until it is crisp-tender; discard any excess water and transfer the boiled broccoli florets to the prepared casserole dish. Scatter the sautéed garlic around the broccoli florets.

4. Drizzle the remaining tablespoon of olive oil; sprinkle the salt, black pepper, and

paprika over your broccoli. Pour in the cream of mushroom soup.

5. Top with the Swiss cheese and bake approximately 18 minutes until the cheese bubbled all over. Bon appétit!

Nutrition: calories: 180 fat: 10.3g protein: 13.5g carbs: 7.6g net carbs: 4.0g fiber: 3.6g

21. Za'atar Chanterelle Stew

Preparation time: 15 minutes

Cooking time: 50 minutes

Servings: 2

Ingredients:

- ½ teaspoon Za'atar spice

- 4 tablespoons olive oil

- ½ cup shallots, chopped

- 2bell peppers, chopped

- 1poblano pepper, finely chopped

- 8 ounces (227 g) Chanterelle mushroom, sliced

- ½ teaspoon garlic, minced

- Sea salt and freshly cracked black pepper, to taste

- 1cup tomato purée

- 3 cups vegetable broth

- 1bay laurel

Directions:

1. Combine the Za'atar with 3 tablespoons of olive oil in a small saucepan. Cook over a moderate flame until hot; make sure not to burn the zaatar. Set aside for 1hour to cool and infuse.

2. In a heavy-bottomed pot, heat the remaining tablespoon of olive oil. Now, sauté the shallots and bell peppers until just tender and fragrant.

3. Stir in the poblano pepper, mushrooms, and garlic; continue to sauté until the mushrooms have softened.

4. Next, add in the salt, black pepper, tomato purée, broth, and bay laurel. Once your stew begins to boil, turn the heat down to a simmer.

5. Let it simmer for about 40 minutes until everything is thoroughly cooked. Ladle into individual bowls and drizzle each serving with Za'atar oil. Bon appétit!

Nutrition: calories: 156 fat: 13.8g protein: 1.4g carbs: 6.0g net carbs: 3.1g fiber: 2.9g

22. Green Cabbage with Tofu

Preparation time: 5 minutes

Cooking time: 15 minutes

Servings: 2

Ingredients:

- 6ounces (170 g) tofu, diced

- ½ shallot, chopped

- 2garlic cloves, finely chopped

- 1(1½-pound / 680-g) head green cabbage, cut into strips

- ½ cup vegetable broth

Directions:

1. Heat up a lightly oiled sauté pan over moderate heat. Now, cook the tofu until brown and crisp; set aside.

2. Then, sauté the shallot and garlic until just tender and fragrant. Add in the green cabbage and beef bone broth; stir to combine.

3. Reduce the heat to medium-low and continue cooking an additional 13 minutes. Season with salt to taste, top with reserved tofu and serve warm. Bon appétit!

Nutrition: calories: 168 fat: 11.7g protein: 10.5g carbs: 5.2g net carbs: 2.9g fiber: 2.3g

DESSERTS

23. Strawberry Dump Cake

Preparation Time: 10 minutes

Cooking Time: 40 minutes

Serve: 12

Ingredients:

- 16 oz. box cake mix

- 20 oz. can pineapple, crushed

- 21/2cups strawberries, frozen, thawed, & sliced

Directions:

1. Add strawberries into the cooking pot and spread evenly.

2. Mix together cake mix and crushed pineapple and pour over sliced strawberries and spread evenly.

3. Cover instant pot aura with lid.

4. Select Bake mode and set the temperature to 350 F and time for 40 minutes.

5. Serve and enjoy.

Nutrition: Calories 175,Fat 2.3 g Carbs: 5 Sugar: 3

24. Baked Apples

Preparation Time: 10 minutes

Cooking Time: 30 minutes

Serve: 6

Ingredients:

- 4 apples, sliced
- 1/2tsp. cinnamon
- 1tbsp. butter, melted

Directions:

1. Toss sliced apples with butter and cinnamon and place them into the cooking pot.

2. Cover instant pot aura with lid.

3. Select Bake mode and set the temperature to 375 F and time for 30 minutes.

4. Serve and enjoy.

Nutrition: Calories 95, Fat 2, Carbs 2, Protein 1

25. Baked Peaches

Preparation Time: 10 minutes

Cooking Time: 10 minutes

Serve: 6

Ingredients:

- 3 ripe peaches, slice in half & remove the

  pit
- 1/4 tsp. cinnamon
- 2tbsp. brown sugar
- 1tbsp. butter

Directions:

1. Mix together butter, brown sugar, and cinnamon and place in the middle of each peach piece.

2. Place peaches in the cooking pot.

3. Cover instant pot aura with lid.

4. Select Bake mode and set the temperature to 375 F and time for 10 minutes.

5. Serve and enjoy.

Nutrition:

Calories 158,

Fat 12,

Carbs 4,

Protein 11

26. Delicious Peach Crisp

Preparation Time: 10 minutes

Cooking Time: 45 minutes

Serve: 8

Ingredients:

- 8 cups can peach, sliced

- 1/2cup butter, cubed

- 1/2cup brown sugar

- 1/2cup all-purpose flour

- 11/2cups rolled oats

- 2tbsp. cornstarch

- 1/2cup sugar

Directions:

1. Add peaches, cornstarch, and sugar into the cooking pot and stir well.

2. Mix together butter, brown sugar, flour, and oats and sprinkle over peaches.

3. Cover instant pot aura with lid.

4. Select Bake mode and set the temperature to 350 F and time for 30-45 minutes.

5. Serve with ice cream

Nutrition: Calories 478, Fat 12, Carbs 3.7, Protein 3

27. Gingerbread Pudding Cake

Preparation Time: 10 minutes

Cooking Time: 2hours 30 minutes

Serve: 6

Ingredients:

- 1egg

- 11/4 cups whole wheat flour

- 1/8 tsp. ground nutmeg

- 1/2tsp. ground ginger

- 1/2tsp. ground cinnamon

- 3/4 tsp. baking soda

- 1cup of water

- 1/2cup molasses

- 1tsp. vanilla

- 1/4 cup sugar

- 1/4 cup butter, softened

- 1/4 tsp. salt

Directions:

1. In a bowl, beat sugar and butter until combined. Add egg and beat until combined.

2. Add water, molasses, and vanilla and beat until well combined.

3. Add flour, nutmeg, ginger, cinnamon, baking soda, and salt and stir until combined.

4. Pour batter into the cooking pot.

5. Cover instant pot aura with lid.

6. Select slow cook mode and cook on HIGH for 21/2hours.

7. Serve with vanilla ice-cream.

Nutrition: Calories 278, Fat 8, Carbs 4.9, Protein 3

CPSIA information can be obtained
at www.ICGtesting.com
Printed in the USA
BVHW042341260621
610451BV00004B/946